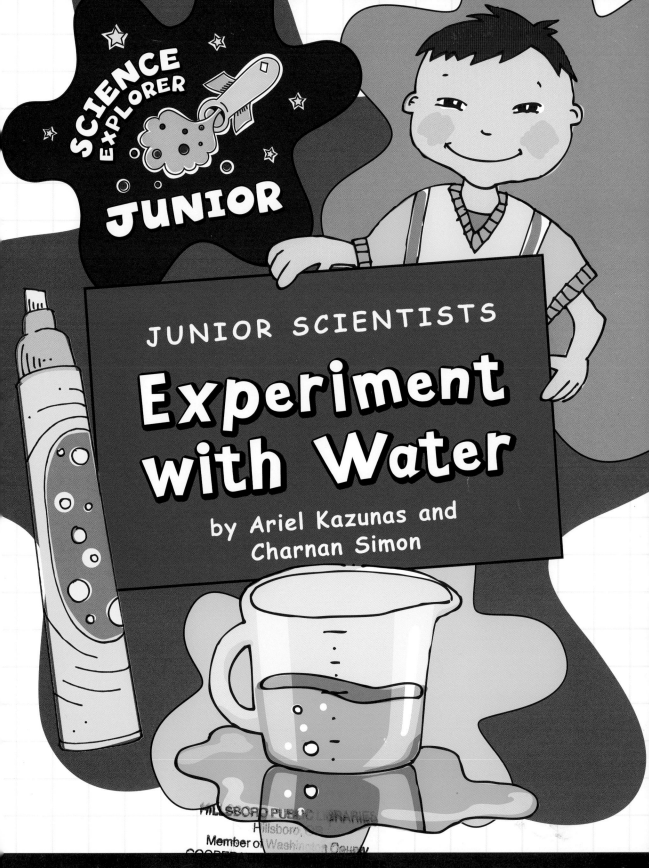

SCIENCE EXPLORER JUNIOR

JUNIOR SCIENTISTS

Experiment with Water

by Ariel Kazunas and Charnan Simon

CHERRY LAKE PUBLISHING · ANN ARBOR, MICHIGAN

NOTE TO PARENTS AND TEACHERS: Please review the instructions for these experiments before your children do them. Be sure to help them with any experiments you do not think they can safely conduct on their own.

NOTE TO KIDS: Be sure to ask an adult for help with these experiments. Always put your safety first!

Published in the United States of America by Cherry Lake Publishing
Ann Arbor, Michigan
www.cherrylakepublishing.com

Content Editor: Robert Wolffe, EdD, Professor of Teacher Education, Bradley University, Peoria, Illinois
Reading Adviser: Cecilia Minden-Cupp, PhD, Literacy Consultant

Design and Illustration: The Design Lab

Photo Credits: Page 15, ©Sue Robinson/Shutterstock, Inc.; page 16, ©Jlye/Dreamstime.com; page 21, ©Rick Lord/Shutterstock, Inc.; page 22, ©anistidesign/Shutterstock, Inc.; page 27, ©Vesilvio/Dreamstime.com; page 28, ©Zsolt Nyulaszi/Shutterstock, Inc.

Library of Congress Cataloging-in-Publication Data
Simon, Charnan.
  Junior scientists: experiment with water / by Charnan Simon and Ariel Kazunas.
      p. cm.—(Science explorer junior)
  Includes bibliographical references and index.
  ISBN-13: 978-1-60279-838-0 (lib. bdg.)
  ISBN-10: 1-60279-838-9 (lib. bdg.)
  1. Water—Experiments—Juvenile literature. I. Kazunas, Ariel. II. Title.
III. Series.
  GB662.3.S54 2010
  532.0078—dc22   2009048821

Portions of the text have previously appeared in *Super Cool Science Experiments: Water* published by Cherry Lake Publishing.

Cherry Lake Publishing would like to acknowledge the work of The Partnership for 21st Century Skills. Please visit *www.21stcenturyskills.org* for more information.

Printed in the United States of America
Corporate Graphics Inc.
July 2010
CLFA07

TABLE OF CONTENTS

Let's Experiment!

Science is fun!

Have you ever done a science **experiment**? They can be a lot of fun! You can use experiments to learn about almost anything.

Good scientists observe the world around them.

This book will help you learn how to think like a scientist. Scientists have a special way of learning new things. Some people call it the Scientific Method. This is how it often works:

- Scientists notice things. They **observe** the world around them. They ask questions about things they see, hear, taste, touch, or smell. They come up with problems they would like to solve.

A scientist guesses the answer to her question.

- They gather information. They use what they already know to guess the answers to their questions. This kind of guess is called a **hypothesis**.

- Then they test their ideas. They perform experiments or build models. They watch and write down what happens. They learn from each new test.

Scientists perform experiments to answer their questions.

- They think about what they learned and reach a **conclusion**. This means they come up with an answer to their question. Sometimes they conclude that they need to do more experiments!

Conclusion

When a scientist figures out the answer to her question, she has reached a conclusion.

Get ready to see water through the eyes of a scientist!

We will think like scientists to learn more about water. We need water to live. We drink it every day. We use water to stay clean, too.

Have you ever had questions about water? What happens when water gets very hot? There are many questions we can ask about water. We'll run experiments to answer them. Each experiment will teach us something about water. Are you ready to be a scientist?

Thin Skin

Science is everywhere, even in a raindrop!

What do we already know about water? Think about a falling raindrop. The drop often stays in one piece instead of breaking apart. The tiny parts that make up water stick together, almost like magnets.

Water drops pull on the water around them. Picture the water on the top of a lake. It pulls even harder on the water next to and below it. This is because there is no water above it. The surface of the water acts like a skin. This is called **surface tension**.

Is it possible to make surface tension weaker? Maybe we could do it by adding something to the water. What happens if we add soap? Let's experiment to find out. First, choose a hypothesis:

1. Adding soap to water weakens surface tension.
2. Adding soap to water does not weaken surface tension.

Let's get started!

Write down your hypothesis.

Adding soap to water . . .

Here's what you'll need:

- 2 clear glasses
- A spoon
- A bowl of water
- Liquid dishwashing soap
- A small loop of thread

Collect your supplies.

Instructions:

1. Fill a glass almost to the top with water. Place it on a flat table.

2. Use the spoon to add water from the bowl to the glass. Do this very slowly! Add a little water at a time. Get the water to bulge up above the top of the glass. But don't let the water spill over. This is surface tension at work!

You'll need a steady hand for this experiment.

You don't need much soap to see results.

3. Carefully drop a bit of liquid soap on top of the water. What happens?

4. Fill the second glass with water. Don't fill it as high as the first glass.

5. Wet the small loop of thread. Place it on top of the water in the glass. Write down your observations. What does the thread loop look like?

6. Put a drop of soap in the middle of the loop. Don't let any soap touch the thread. Don't let it touch the water outside of the loop, either. Watch carefully. Write down what you notice.

Conclusion:

Soap makes surface tension weaker. What happened when you added the soap to the first glass?

How can we explain what happened to the thread loop's shape? Soap weakened the surface tension in the loop. The surface tension outside the loop didn't change. Why? It did not touch the soap. The water around the loop pulled on the string. Did you prove your hypothesis?

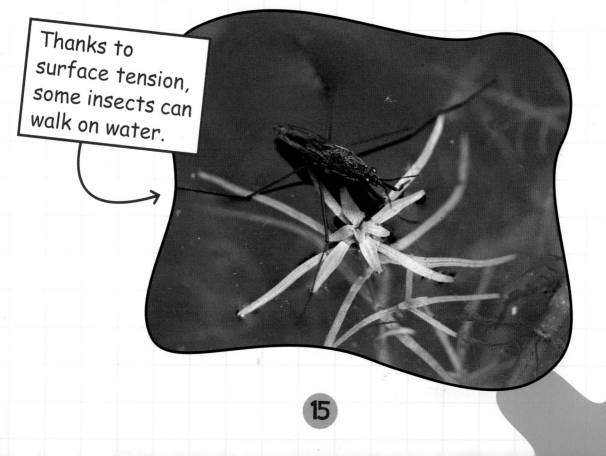

Thanks to surface tension, some insects can walk on water.

Water on the Move

Can water change into a form other than the ones in this glass?

Do you use ice cubes to keep your drinks cold? You know that ice cubes are made of very cold water. What happens when you freeze water? It changes into ice. What happens to water that gets very hot? Does it change into something different? An experiment will help us find out. Choose a hypothesis:

1. Water will change into something else when it gets very hot.
2. Water will not change when it gets very hot.

Let's get started!

Record your hypothesis.

Here's what you'll need:

- An adult helper
- A wooden ruler
- Water
- A saucepan
- A stove

You'll find most of the supplies for this experiment in your kitchen.

This experiment has a simple setup.

Instructions:

1. Pour 3 inches (7.6 centimeters) of water into the pan. Use the ruler to help measure how deep the water is. Write this number down.

2. Have an adult heat the water over a stove. Be careful not to burn yourself! Pay attention. Is the water getting hot? Is it starting to boil? Do you see steam coming out of the pan?

3. Let the water boil for 10 to 15 minutes. Have the adult remove the pan from the stove.

4. Let the water cool. Then use the ruler to measure the water level again.

Has the water level changed?

Do you see the water vapor escaping?

Conclusion:

Was there less water in the pan by the end of the experiment? Where did the water go? When water heats up enough, it turns into steam! Steam is also known as **water vapor**. Water vapor is water in the form of a gas. Did you prove your hypothesis?

Water, Water Everywhere!

Does the bathroom mirror fog up after you take a shower?

We learned that liquid water can become water vapor. We also know that ice melts when it gets warm. This means it turns back into liquid water.

Do you think you can turn water vapor into a liquid? Water vapor forms when water is heated enough. What happens if we cool off the water vapor? It's time for another experiment! Start by choosing a hypothesis:

1. Cooling water vapor will turn it back into a liquid.
2. Cooling water vapor will not turn it back into a liquid.

Let's get started!

Don't forget to write down what you think might happen.

Cooling water vapor will turn it back into a liquid.

Here's what you'll need:

- An adult helper
- Water
- A stove
- A saucepan with a lid

You'll need many of the same supplies you used for Experiment #2.

24

Don't forget to place the lid on the saucepan.

Instructions:

1. Fill the pan halfway with water.
2. Cover the pan with the lid.

Record your results.

3. Have an adult heat the pan over a stove. Be careful around the hot stove!

4. Remove the lid after 15 to 20 minutes. Is steam coming from the pan? Look at the bottom of the lid. What do you see?

Conclusion:

Was the bottom of the lid covered with drops of water? Why do you think this is? The vapor rose up as the water got hot enough. It cooled down as it hit the pan's lid. When the water vapor cooled, it turned back into liquid water! This is called **condensation**. Did you prove your hypothesis?

Water vapor is at work inside this steamer.

Do It Yourself!

What experiments will you think up next?

Okay, scientists! Now you know more about water. You learned it all through your observations and experiments.

Do you have other questions about water? How cold does water have to get before it freezes? Is it possible to get the salt out of salt water? Put the scientific method to use and find out!

GLOSSARY

conclude (kuhn-KLOOD) to make a final decision based on what you know

conclusion (kuhn-KLOO-zhuhn) a final decision, thought, or opinion

condensation (kon-den-SAY-shuhn) the act of changing from a gas to a liquid or solid

experiment (ecks-PARE-uh-ment) a scientific way to test a guess about something

hypothesis (hy-POTH-uh-sihss) a guess about what will happen in an experiment

method (METH-uhd) a way of doing something

observe (uhb-ZURV) to see something or notice things with the other senses

surface tension (SUR-fiss TEN-shuhn) a force that allows the surface of water to have a stretchy "skin"

water vapor (WAW-tur VAY-pur) water in the form of a gas

FOR MORE INFORMATION

BOOKS

Just Add Water: Science Experiments You Can Sink, Squirt, Splash, Sail. New York: Children's Press, 2008.

Korb, Rena. *The Wild Water Cycle*. Edina, MN: Magic Wagon, 2008.

WEB SITES

EPA Environmental Kids Club—The Water Cycle
www.epa.gov/safewater/kids/flash/
flash_watercycle.html
Check out this clip and learn about the water cycle.

National Geographic Kids—Quiz Your Noodle!: Water
kids.nationalgeographic.com/Games/PuzzlesQuizzes/
Quizyournoodle-water
Put your smarts to the test and learn more about water!

INDEX

ABOUT THE AUTHORS

Charnan Simon is a former editor of *Cricket* magazine and the author of more than 100 books for young readers. She lives in Seattle, Washington, where there is a lot of water.

Ariel Kazunas is a writer who has worked for several nonprofit magazines. She is also a kayak guide and instructor, which explains her love of all things having to do with water.